Sit & Solve
MAZES

THE DIAGRAM GROUP

Sterling Publishing Co., Inc. New York

A Diagram Book first created by Diagram Visual Information Limited
of 195 Kentish Road, London NW5 2JU, England

12 14 16 18 20 19 17 15 13

Published by Sterling Publishing Co., Inc.
387 Park Avenue South, New York, N.Y. 10016
Includes material previously published under the title
The Little Giant Encyclopedia of Mazes
© 1976, 2002 by Diagram Visual Information Ltd.
Distributed in Canada by Sterling Publishing
c/o Canadian Manda Group, 165 Dufferin Street,
Toronto, Ontario, Canada M6K 3H6
Distributed in Great Britain by Chrysalis Books Group PLC,
The Chrysalis Building, Bramley Road, London W10 6SP, England
Distributed in Australia by Capricorn Link (Australia) Pty. Ltd.
P.O. Box 704, Windsor, NSW 2756 Australia

Printed in China

Sterling ISBN 0-8069-8867-3

For information about custom editions, special sales, premium and
corporate purchases, please contact Sterling Special Sales
Department at 800-805-5489 or specialsales@sterlingpub.com

CONTENTS

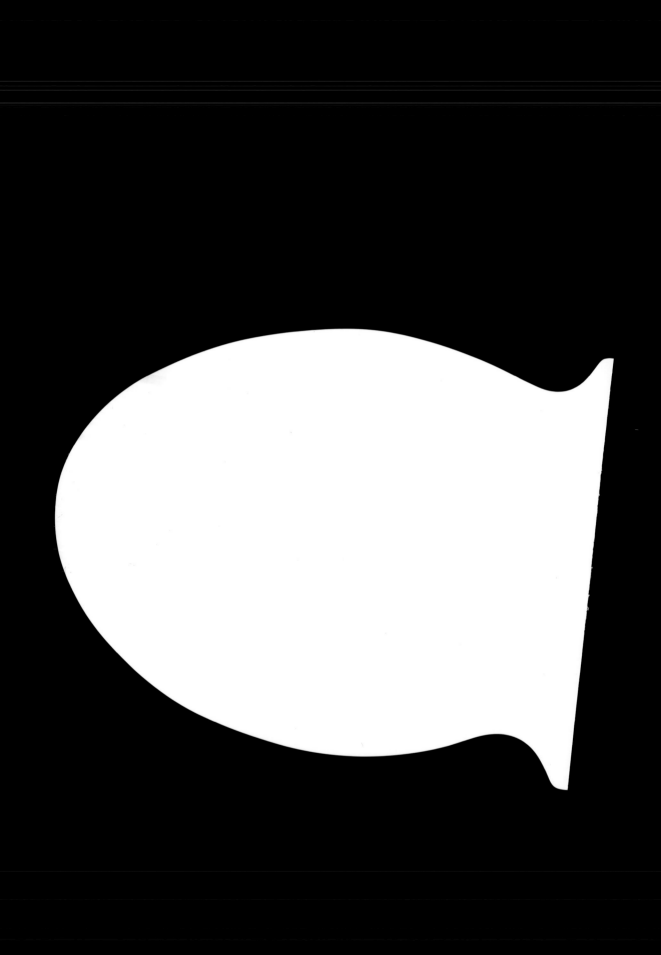

INTRODUCTION

Tired of reading? Fed up with words? In need of visual stimulation?

Then this book is for you. *Sit & Solve Mazes* contains 45 puzzles designed to confuse, daze, and bewilder, but above all, to entertain

Some mazes look simple to solve; others are more complex. Many are intricate labyrinths with netwoks of winding pathways leading to perplexing blind alleys.

This book will give you and your family hours of enjoyment.

To solve a maze, find the shortest route from A to B through the maze. If you get stuck, you can always peek at the answers in the back of the book.

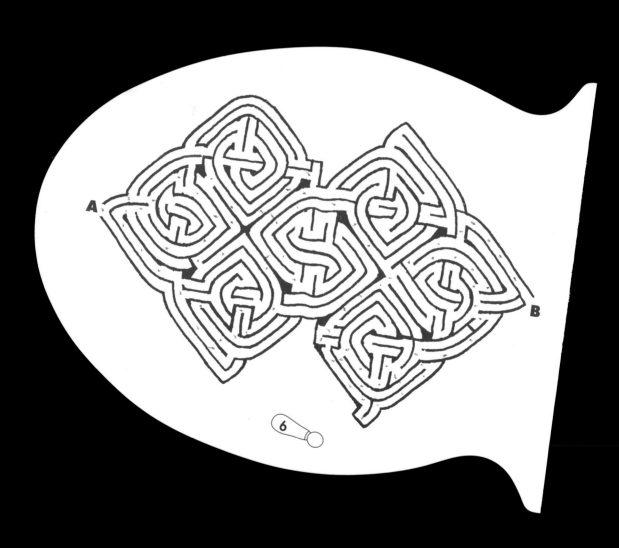

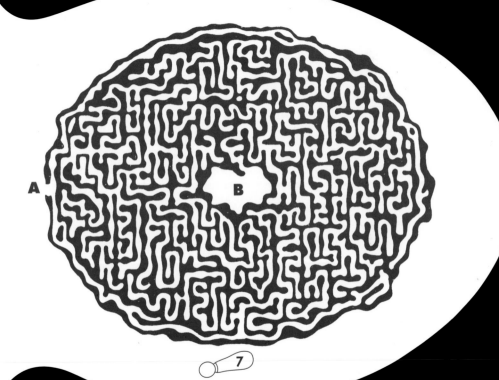

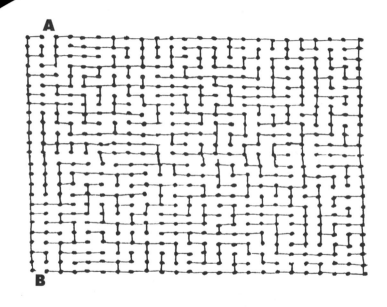

A

B

8

9

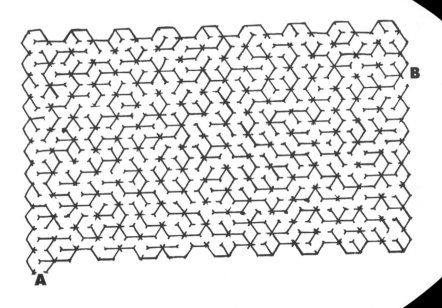

A

B

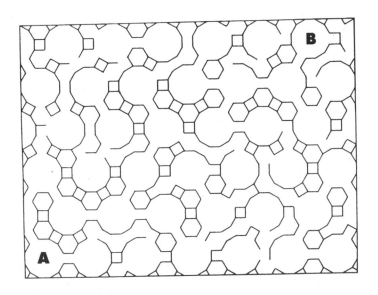

15

A

B

16

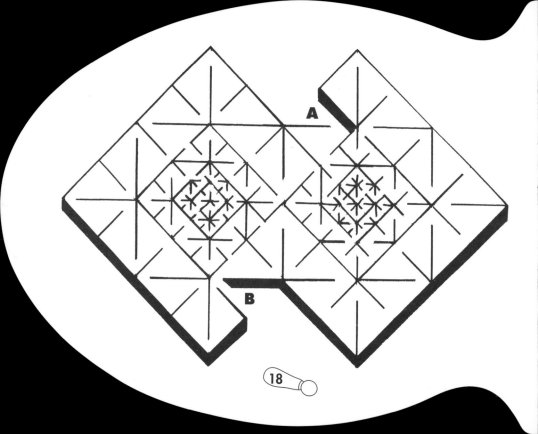

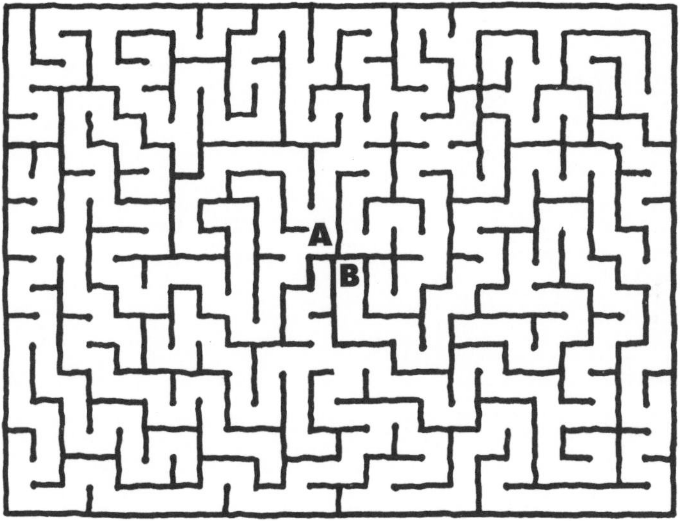
A
B

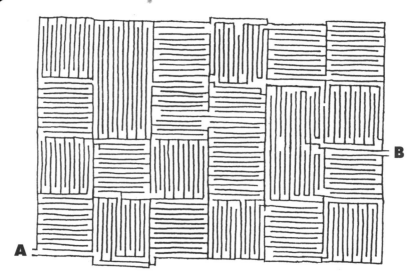

A

B

20

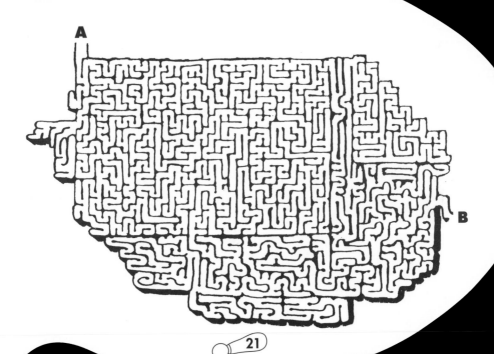

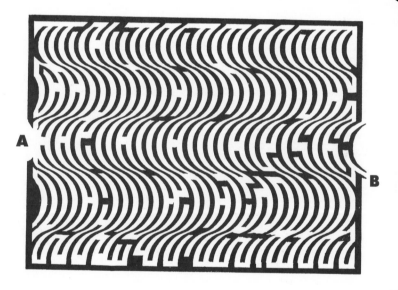

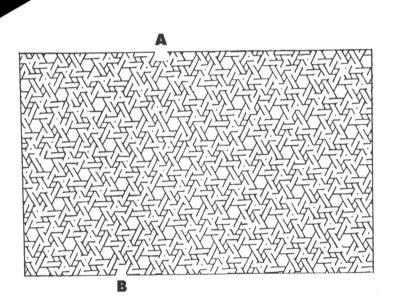

A

B

26

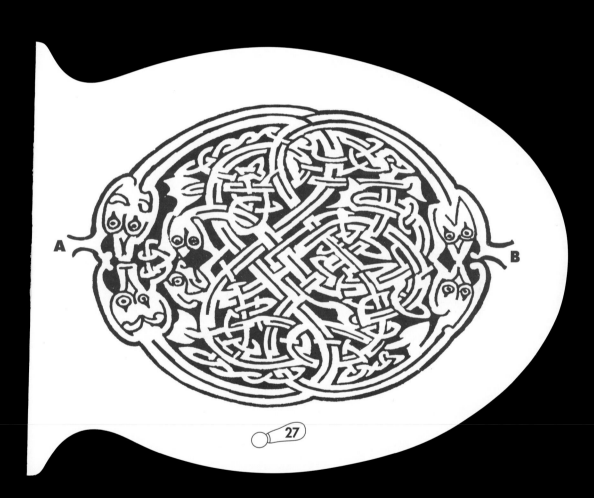

A

B

27

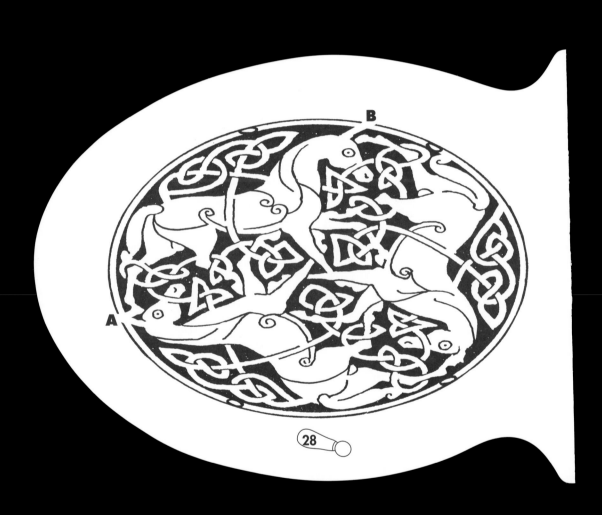

A

B

29

A

B

30

A

B

33

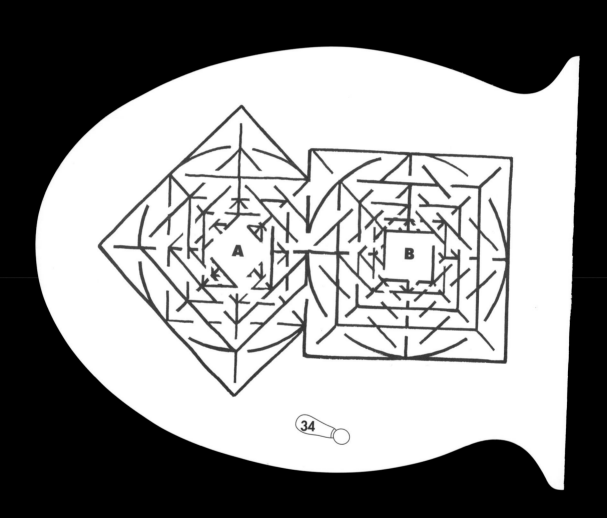

34

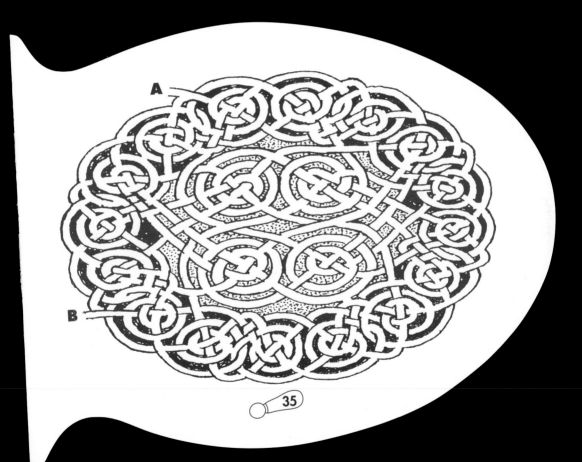

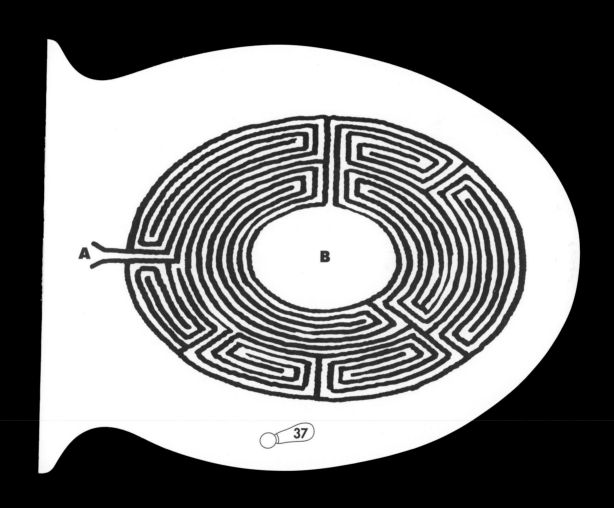

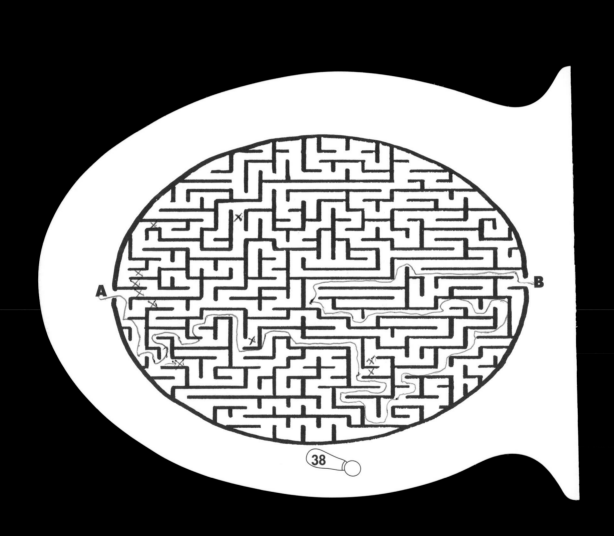

38

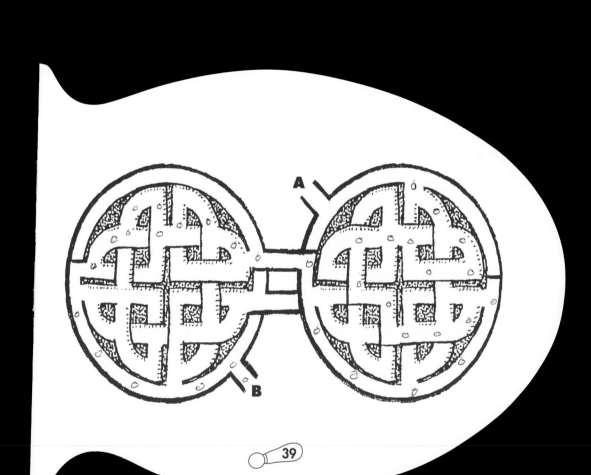

42

A

B

43

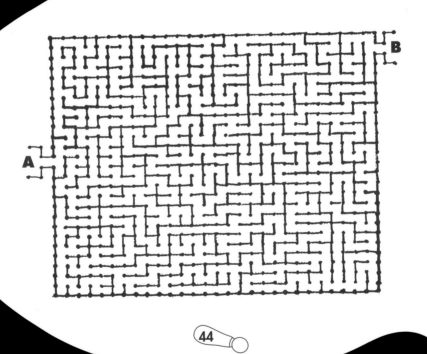

44

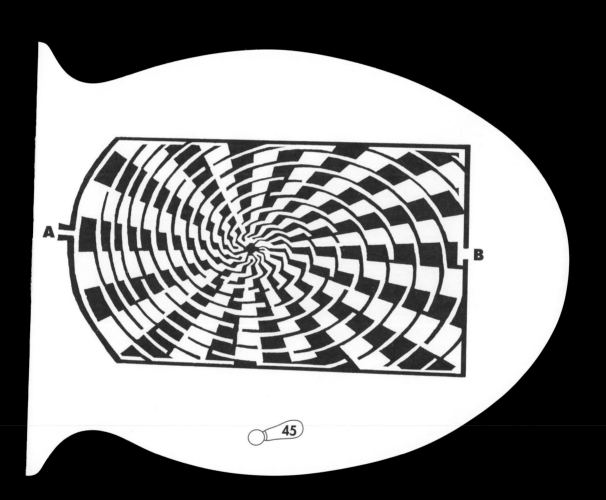

A

B

45

A

B

46

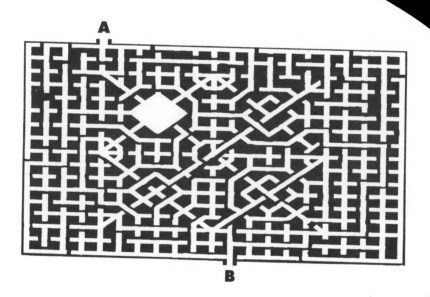

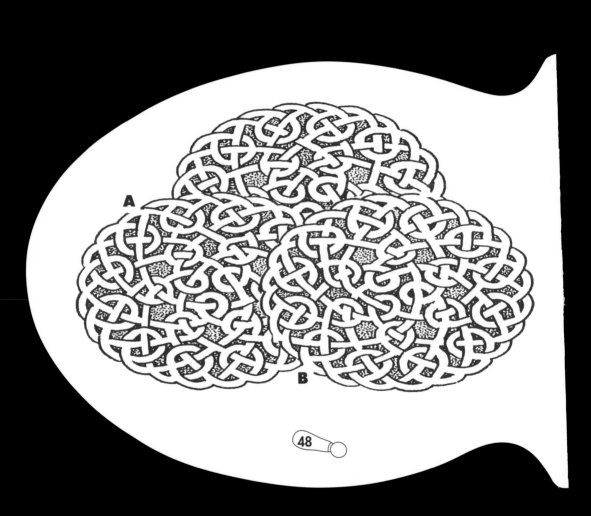

48

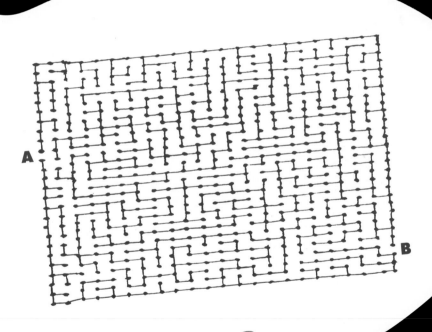

A

B

49

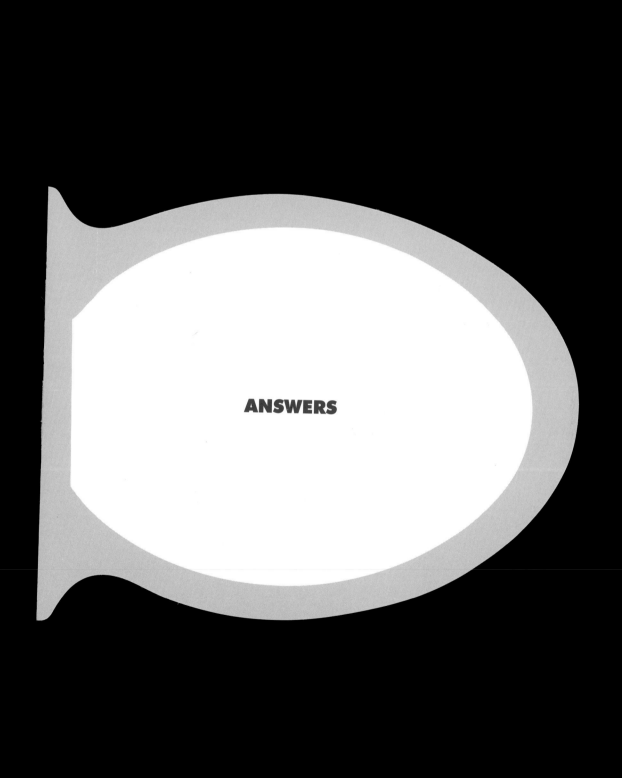

ANSWERS

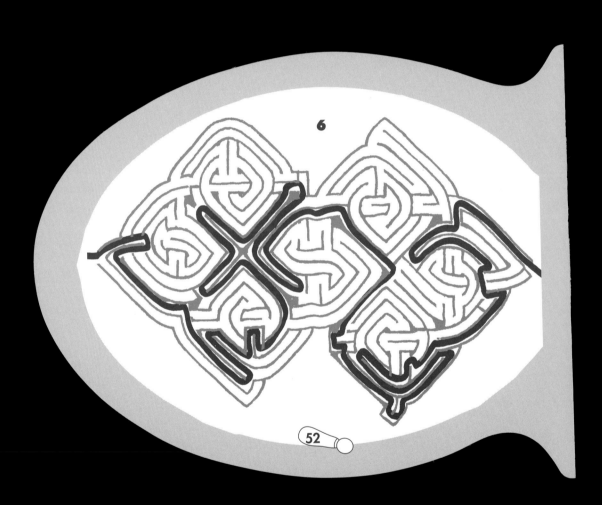

6

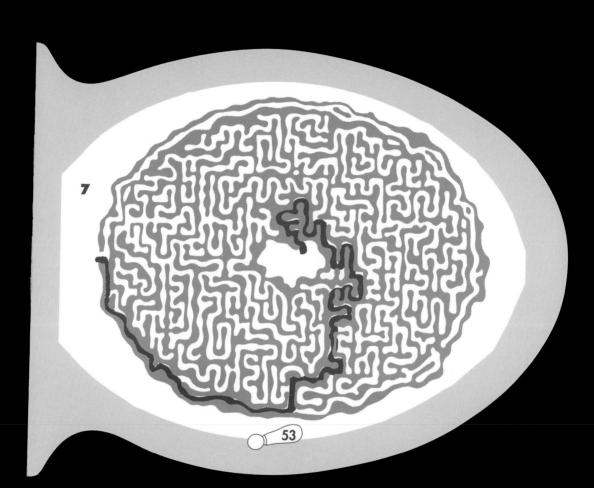

7

53

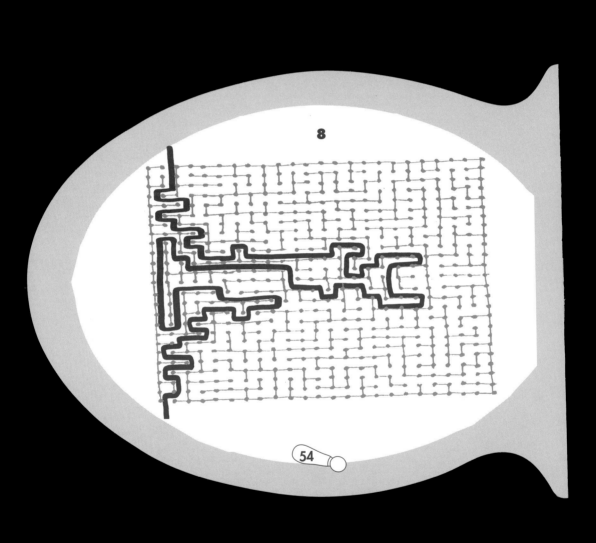

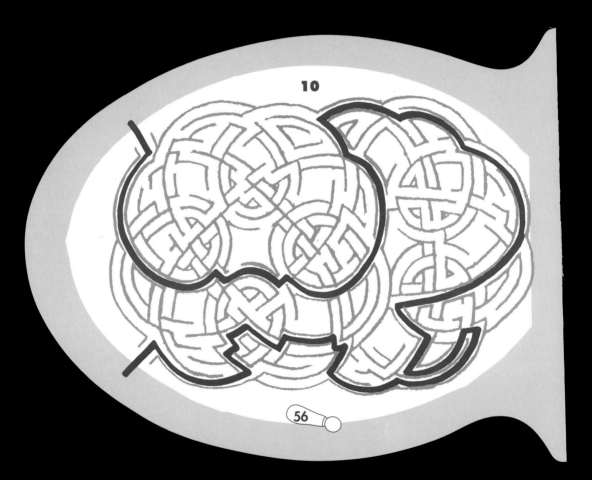

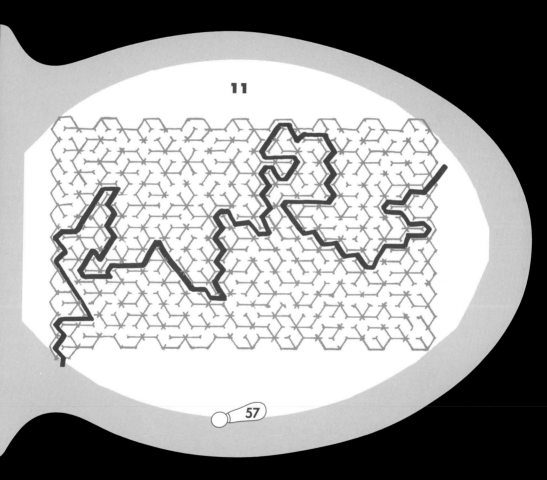

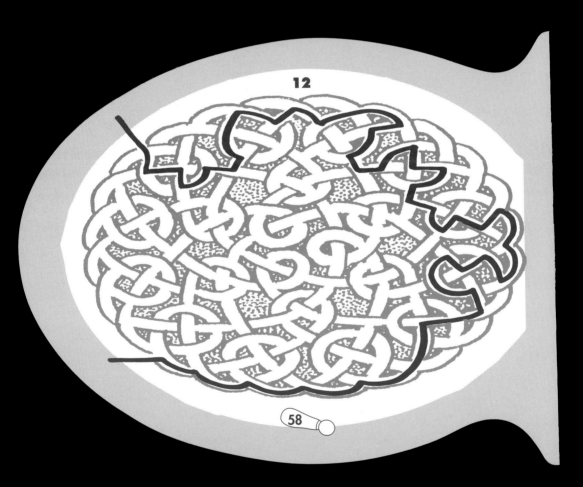

58

13

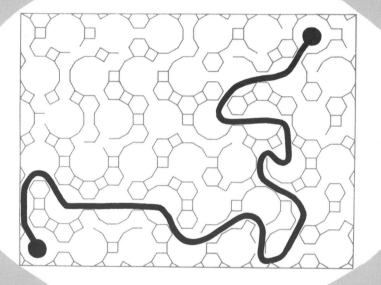

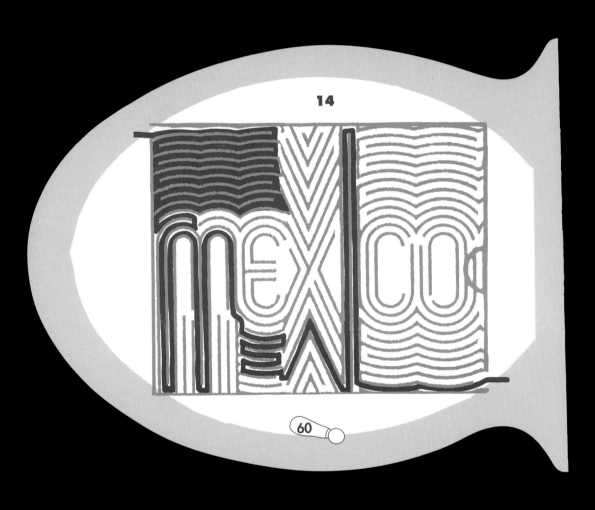

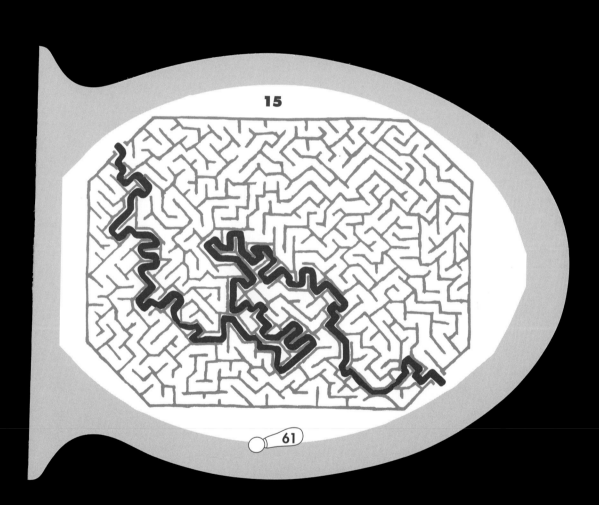

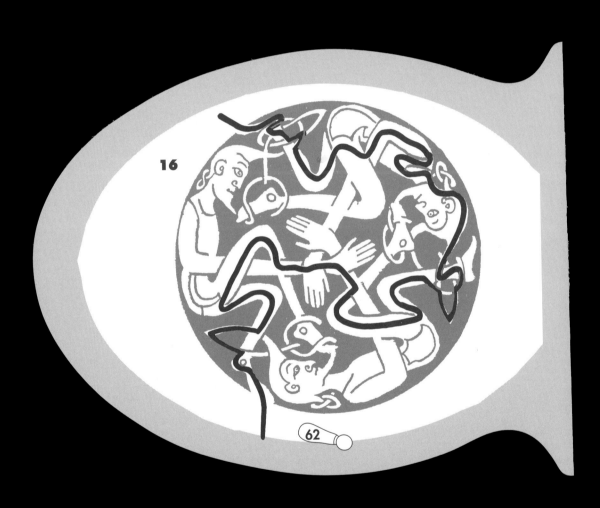

16

62

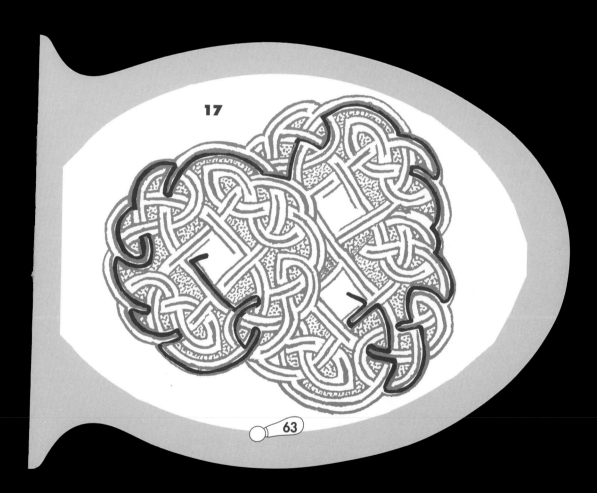

17

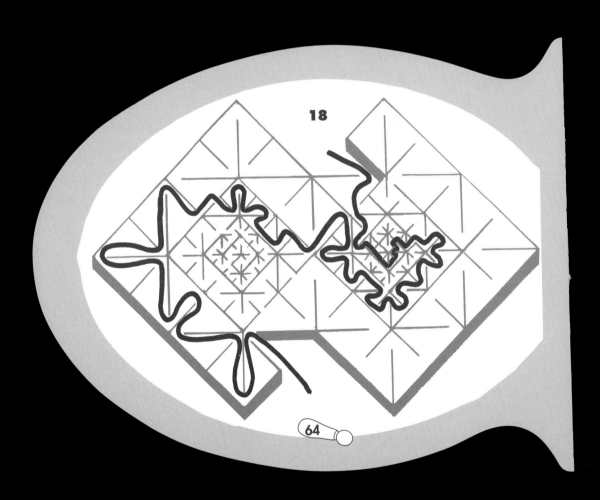

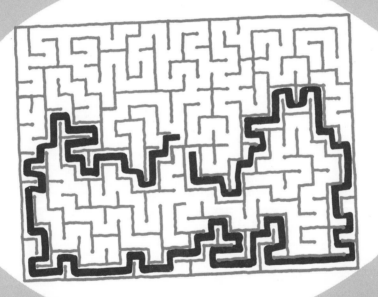

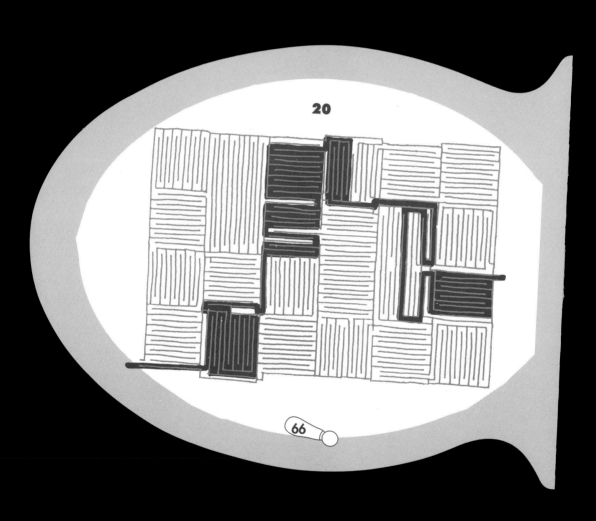

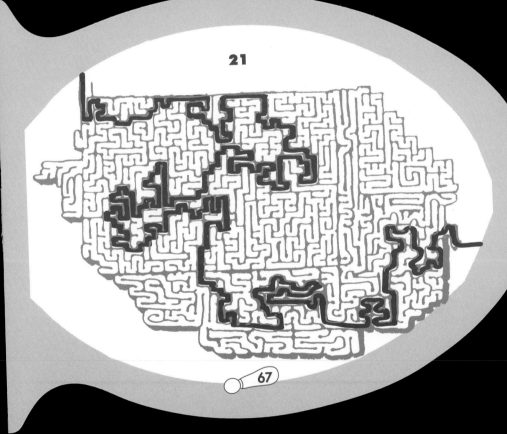

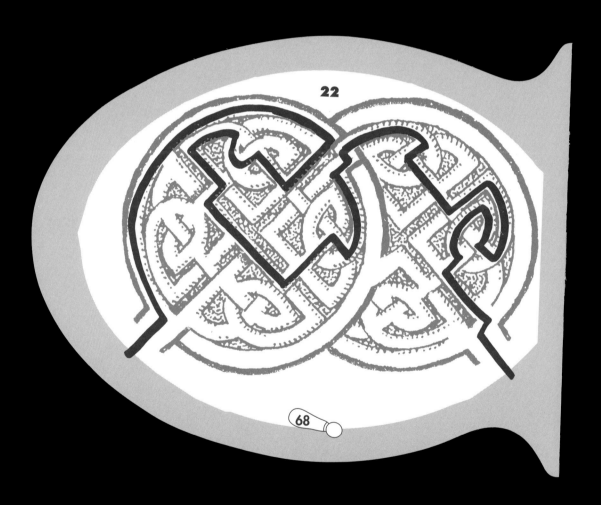

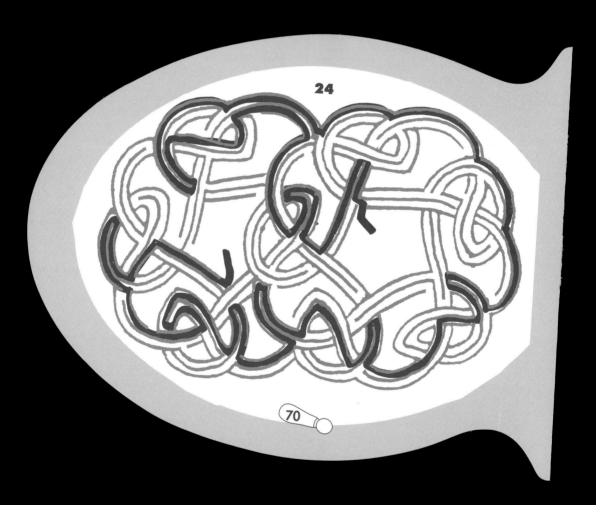

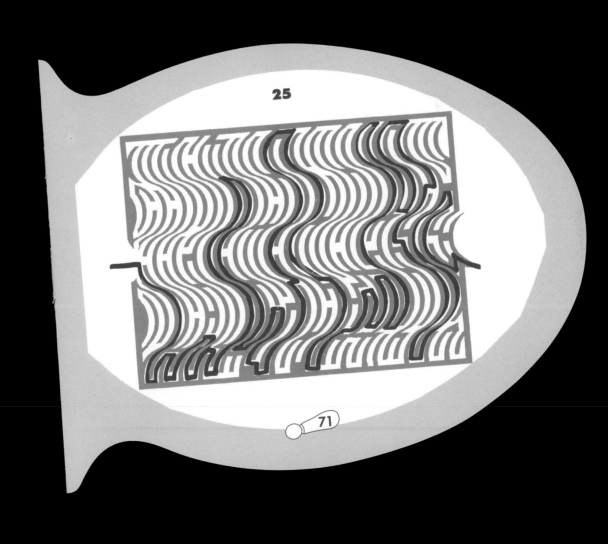

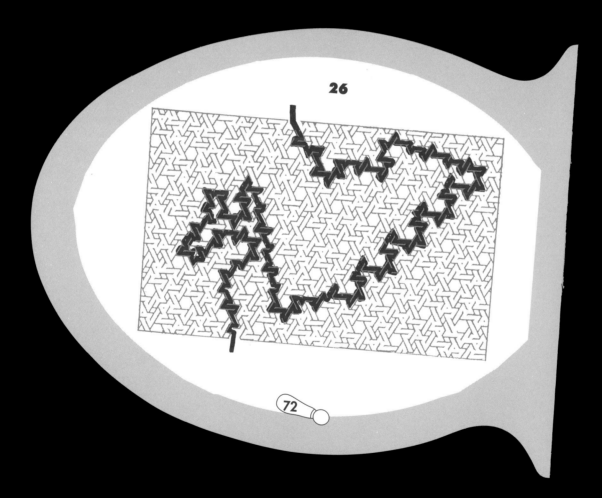

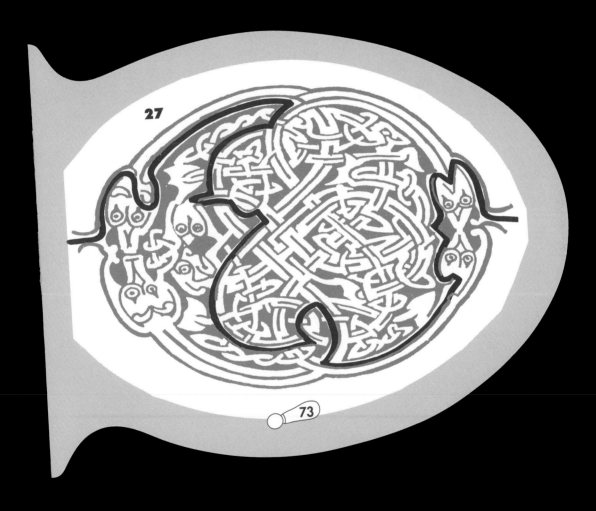

27

73

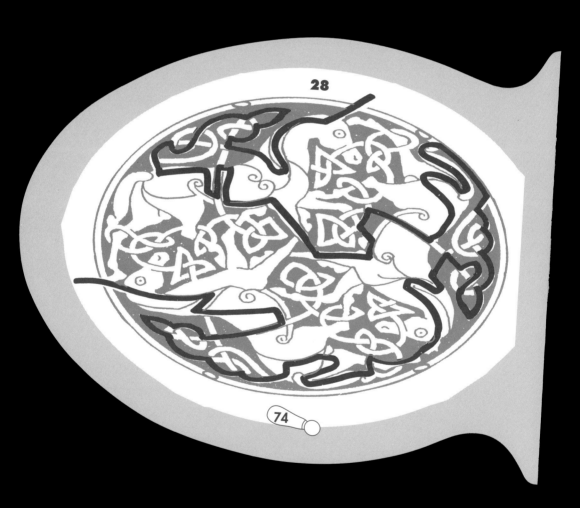

28

74

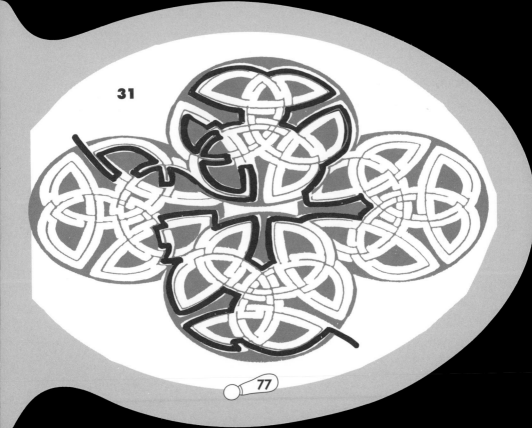

31

33

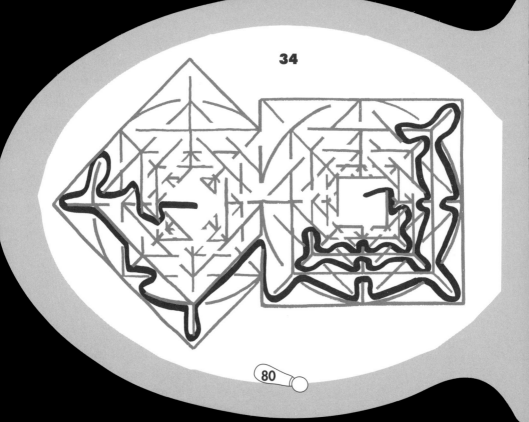

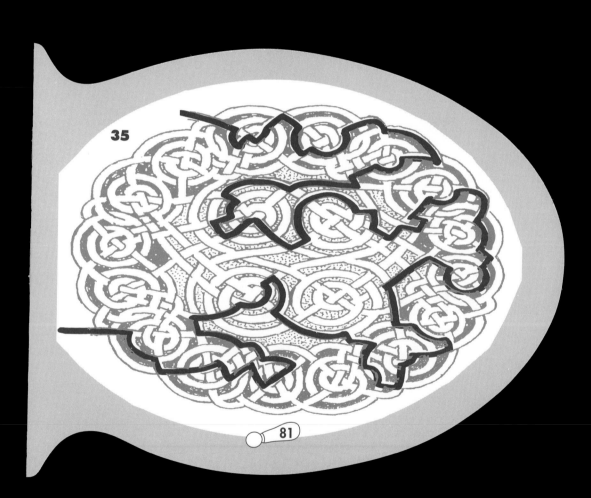

35

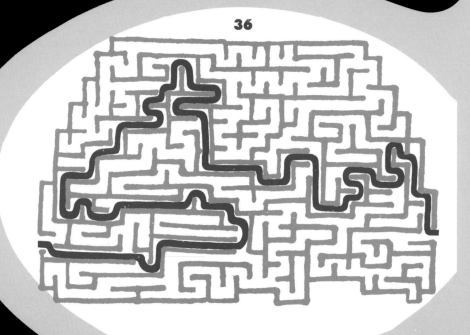

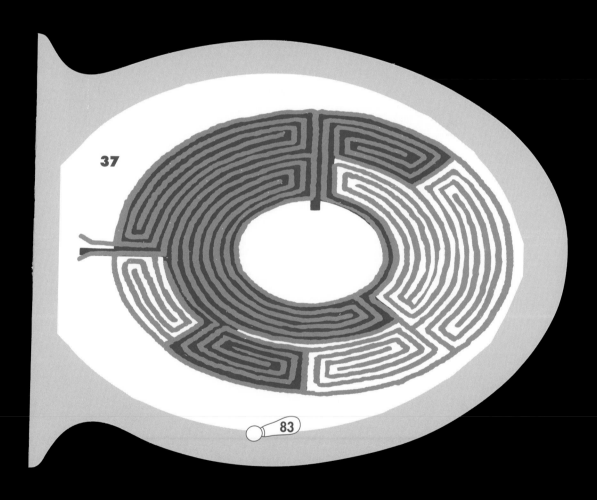

37

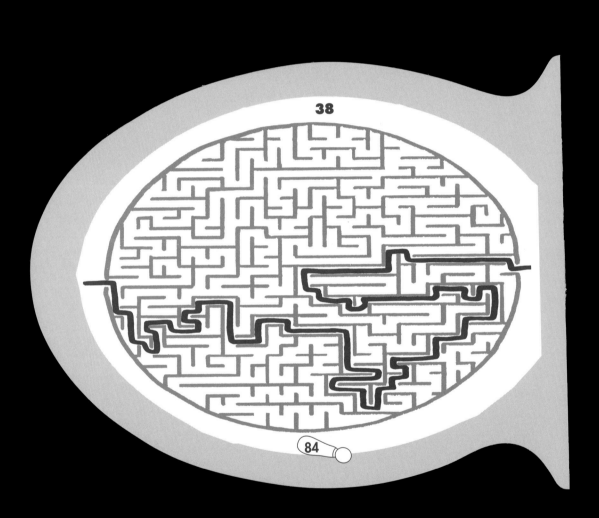

84

39

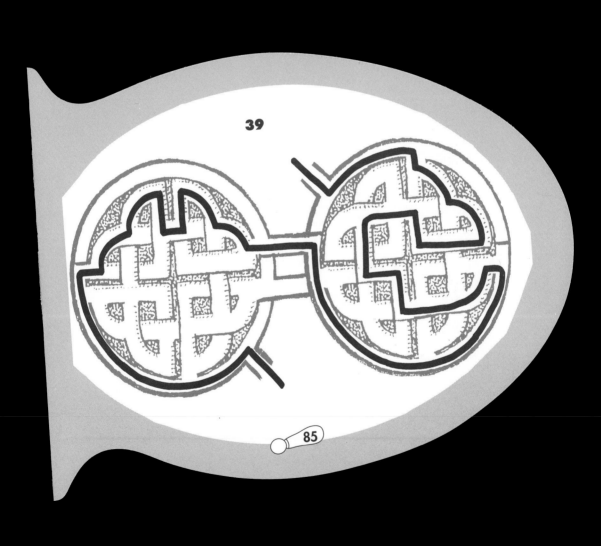

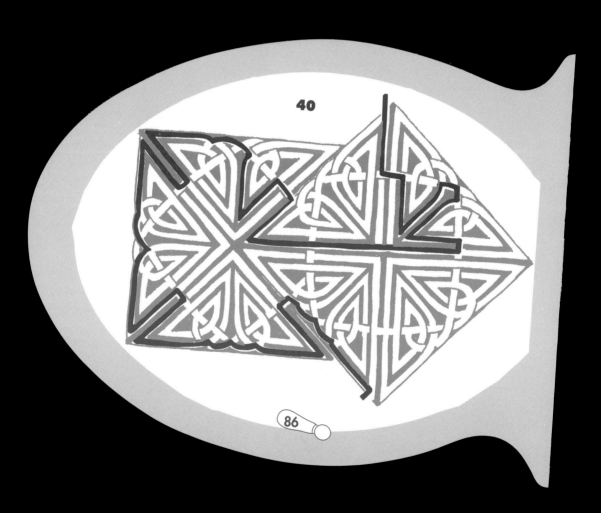

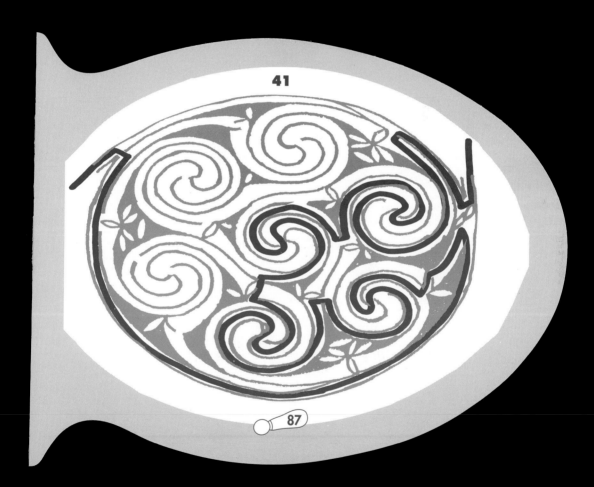

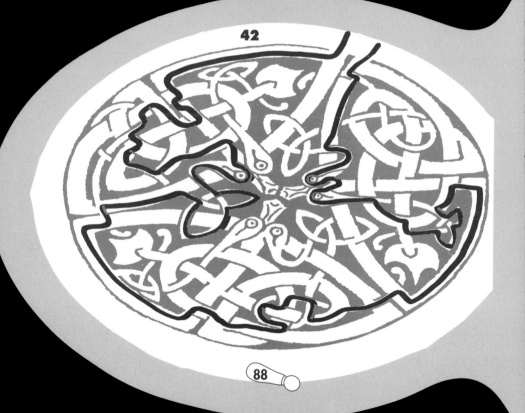

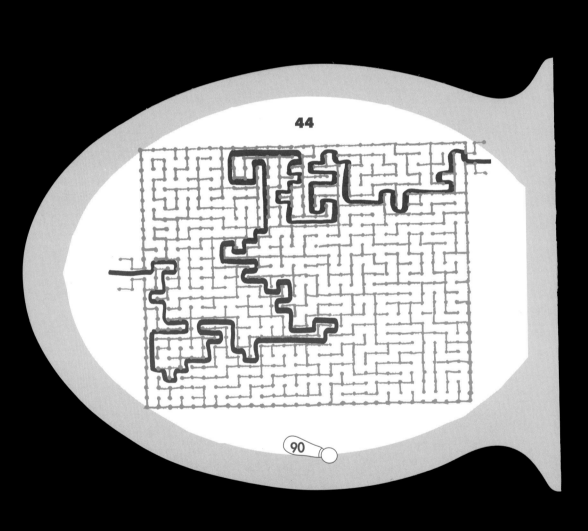